With God, I Did It

a Memoir

By Dr. Dawn Silvera-Ndure, FNP

Publication Data

Book Cover Photography by Nickeisha Bardowell

Table of Content

Acknowledgement

Introduction

With God, I Did It

a Memoir

By Dr. Dawn Silvera-Ndure, FNP

Acknowledgement

I must first acknowledge the Most High God, the Creator of Heaven and Earth for motivating me to tell the story. He deserves the praise and glory. I would like to take this opportunity to express my gratitude and thanks to my editor Ms. Valerie Adams for motivating me to start the process, advised me while writing and completing my story. In addition I want to thank Ms. Novella Coleman (author, poet, and motivational speaker), Ms. Monica Hay (teacher and friend), Ms. Charlene Rose (teacher and niece) for their assistance in proofreading and offering suggestions on the final manuscript. I give honor to my spiritual Mentors, Archbishop Bernard Jordan, Pastor Debra Jordan, the Zoe ministries family and the company of Prophets for their words of inspiration and spiritual guidance during my life journey. I also want to thank my daughters Velicia Bardowell, Nickeisha Bardowell, Crystal Bardowell, and Destini Bardowell for their support over the years. In addition, I want to thank my Aunt-Florence Hinds, my Brother-Norman Rose, my Sister-Paula Campbell, and my mother, Joycelyn Danvers, as well as friends and other family members for supporting me during every season of my life.

Introduction

Recently, I was home watching a very interesting movie. At the end of the movie, the gospel song, "Worth," began to play. I heard this song before, but today, it spoke to me in a very special way. The presence of God was all over my heart. I felt God speaking to me. It was as if a veil was removed from my eyes and I saw my life as a young child. The words of the song highlight the favor of God. As the song ministered to me I cried and cried. I received a clear revelation as God made me aware that He placed value on my life. That day, I knew God guided my life and led me on the path making me who I am today. The song brought back memories of my childhood and all the events that led to my accomplishments.

I flirted several times with the idea of writing an autobiography but never did. I was given prophetic words about writing "the book." I even received information on the title and cover picture, but I kept putting it off. That day, I became present to the fact that I must tell the story to let others know that God can take the impossible and make all things possible. God can take our weakness and make us strong. He can take our sickness and make us whole. He can take our poverty and create wealth. He allows us to rise out of the darkness of our nothingness and create light and beauty. We are the creators of our world. So, with God by our side, we can accomplish anything. My mentors Archbishop Bernard Jordan and Pastor Debra Jordan reminds us that "Destiny is not a matter of chance, but it is a matter of choice".

Chapter 1: Family History

My mother had me at a tender age. Her family was well known and respected in the community. My maternal grandfather was Theophelus Gordon. He and my grandmother relocated from a town known as Clarkes Town in the parish of Trelawny, Jamaica, and started a life in the town of Little Bay, Port Maria, St. Mary. My grandfather was a man of multiple talents.

He was a known fisherman, a boat maker, and a farmer. He provided for my six uncles and seven aunts. My grandfather died before I was born. My grandmother's name was Celestina Gordon. Her family's name was White. My maternal grandparents had thirteen children, which included three sets of twins. My mother was the 10th born child. The son's names are: Samuel, Phillip, Desmond, Joseph, Noel, and Bunnywell. The daughter's names are Eulalee, Beryl, Audrey, Florence, Gloria, Mavis, and Joycelyn. I have many cousins from my mother's side. We all grew up together as sisters and brothers. Our Bond and love remains very strong to this very day. Some of my cousins are: Shaggy, Pauline, Steve, Baba, Bulus, Carol, Philip, Tony, Marcia, Miriam, Sharon, Gracie, Nancy, Camile, Irving, Billy, Orval, Lukie, Troy, Reagan, and Cynthia.

My grandmother, Celestina Gordon, was a midwife and a Spiritual Healer. My childhood memories of my grandmother are not clear. I don't remember her face. However, one special vision kept coming to me over and over as the years went by. I kept remembering myself and another child sitting with her in the back of a church. She was sitting in the middle of us. I must have been no more than three years old. This memory of her reveals that she took me to church and taught me to love the Lord.

Another memory of my grandmother was of me drinking hominy porridge she would make for me. It was the tastiest porridge I ever had. To date, I love hominy porridge. I was later told she was a very good cook and was employed by influential people in the community. My paternal grandmother's name was Rachel Silvera. Originally, she lived in a little town called Retreat in the parish of St. Mary, Jamaica, then relocated to the town of Little Bay. My paternal grandmother met my grandfather and they birthed four daughters and four sons.

My paternal grandfather's name was George Silvera. The Silvera family migrated from Portugal. My paternal grandfather was the descendant of one of the four Silvera Brothers who came on a ship from Portugal and settled in Jamaica. My grandparents had nine children, four boys, and six girls. My father was the seventh born. The son's names were: Pal, Harold, and Leon. The daughters were affectionately known as: Honey, Sallie, Joyce, Sugar, and Birdie.

My father has two sons and one daughter from another relationship. My brothers are Norris Silvera, and Owen Silvera, and my sister is Nadine Silvera. They were all born in the town of Port Maria, St. Mary. I also have several cousins on my father's side. Today, I remain closely connected to my brothers, my sister and my cousins. My father and his family were richly gifted in the arts and music. One of my uncles was a well-known Jamaican bass player who traveled and played internationally. His name was Harold Silvera. My father, Owen Silvera and his brother, Leon Silvera, were well known Jamaican Ska Artists. They were called "The Silvera Brothers". The Silvera Brothers were famous in the 1960s and onwards. Owen and Leon Silvera had several songs such as, *The Fits is Upon Me Now, Me want me cock, All Day Long You Are On My Mind,* and *Next-door Neighbor* were among my favorites as they performed nationally and internationally. My grandmother, Rachel Silvera, was such a gifted songwriter. She wrote many of the songs that made The Silvera Brothers famous.

Some of my father's sisters were very good dancers. Two sisters, Honey and Sallie, were known for winning dance competitions. The Gordon and Silvera family lived in the parish of St. Mary, known as Little Bay. My father and mother's families were neighbors for many years. The town of Little Bay is a small village by the sea. The people were mostly farmers and fishermen. The women worked in homes as cooks and homemakers. Some of the women also worked in the brazier factory and supermarkets in the Town of Port Maria nearby.

Little Bay is next to the town of Castle Garden. The town of Castle Garden is famous for the hotel call Casa Maria. The very famous English writer, Noel Coward has a guesthouse near the sea in Castle Garden. My uncle worked for Noel Coward for many years. Further up the road is the famous hotel call Trade Winds. This hotel stands on a hill overlooking the ocean and the town of Port Maria. The view includes the Cabbarita Island, located in the town of Paggee. The view from the hotel is breathtaking. Directly facing the hotel is the home of the Blackwell's. One member of this family is

Chris Blackwell, the famous Jamaican producer who discovered Bob Marley. His record label is called Island Records.

My mother's name is Joycelyn Gordon. She was married to David Danvers. She had three daughters and one son from previous relationship. I was the firstborn of four children. I have four daughters. My oldest is Velicia Sancelia. She was born in November like me. Velica has a degree in Psychology and is planning to be a Psychologist. Velicia is also a gifted writer and artist. She writes awesome poems. My second daughter is Nickeisha Samantha. She is a gifted singer, songwriter, and artist. She was awarded musical recognition throughout elementary and high school. She even won a gold medal in the *Prestigious NAACP Music Award* for high school students in Westchester, New York. She is presently studying Computer Technology and also writing and producing songs in her home-studio.

My third daughter is Crystal Rene. Crystal has a degree in Early Childhood Education. She is a gifted singer and even tried her hands at songwriting. She loves to travel. In 2016, she traveled to Ireland and shared pictures and videos of awesome sceneries during her stay. My youngest daughter, Destini Marie bears my middle name. Destini is a gifted writer and singer. She loves to write stories. Destini is currently seeking a degree in Early Childhood Education as well. Like myself, my daughters are very sensitive to social causes. We all love animals. We have three awesome dogs; a Labrador-Chow called Prince, a Brindle named Brody, and a small Maltese-shih Tzu called CJ.

My sister, Marcia, was the second born. Marcia is a socialite. She is gifted in having events and social functions in her town of *Mason Hall*. She is well known in her community. Marcia has one daughter, Marissa. Marissa received a scholarship to high school at a very young age. She recently graduated from high school. My sister Paula, affectionately known as Debby, is the third born child. Debby is married to Carlton Campbell, affectionately known as Bampy. Carton is a very dedicated and ambitious father and husband. He worked on cruise ships for many years to provide for his family. They have a beautiful house in the town of *Race Course*, overlooking the sea. My sister's husband made his transition while I was in the process of writing this book. This was one of the saddest days of our life. He died from the complication of diabetes. To date we mourn his sudden passing. I was unable to attend the funeral for our beloved

"Bampie" but through technology I was connected to the speaker system at the church as I performed by phone one of Whitney Houston's song, "I look to you"

My sister Debby and her husband Carlton, has two brilliant and gifted daughters. Both daughters are very good dancers. While growing up, they were usually the center of attention at family parties and other functions because of their dancing ability. The first-born daughter is called Nihal. She is currently studying to be a nutritionist at a University in Kingston, Jamaica. My second niece Nickeal recently graduated from high school and is currently attending Mico College. Debby is a very gifted cosmetologist. She is the CEO and owner of *Debby's Beauty Salon*. She is a gifted businesswoman with an astute mind. She is the one we depend on to take care of our business plans in Jamaica.

My brother Norman, known as Dwight, is the youngest child of my mother. Dwight is married to Sophia, a warm and beautiful person. They have one son named, Sanjay. He is industrious and loves to build things. He is currently in school studying Hotel Hospitality. Dwight has two other children. The first child is Charlene. She is a teacher, very ambitious, and gifted intellectual. Her mother passed at a very young age when she was just a small child. With the support of my mother, her father, and other family members, Charlene overcame the odds and came through the storm. She has an eight-year-old son named Taquan. He surpasses his biological age and excels intellectually. Dwight's second child is Sharlon. He is married to Amanda and they have two children. Sharlon works in a scientific research plant and Amanda is a brilliant teacher.

Sharlon and Amanda's first-born is Angelina. She is a beautiful seven-year-old and Aidan is their cute and smart four-year-old son. My brother, Dwight, is one of the people who motivated me to complete my doctorate degree. He always believed in me. I am so very proud of my brother, and always admired his ambitious personality. For many years he worked very hard on various cruise lines, and with the help of the family he built a beautiful home overlooking the sea in town of Galina, St. Mary. His neighbors are prominent politicans and wealthy business men.

Chapter 2: My Childhood

I have vivid memories of my life as a child. I remember being with my cousins, who were like brothers and sisters to me, on the beach, in the river, and at the fruit orchard in my community. I was an ardent swimmer and diver at an early age. I have memories of diving and swimming in the waters of Little Bay Beach. I remember diving many feet under the water and looking at the water surface above me. I also remember sitting on the rocks all by myself while fishing in the deep waters below me. I even have scars on my knees from falling on the sea rocks while fishing.

Today, I think about how dangerous it was for me. Yet, I was kept safe by the hand of God who guided me. I was like a tomboy. I could play marble games and cricket matches better than anyone. My aunt Audrey, known as Aunty Biggest, was a mother to us all and a great cook. I remember eating the delicious meals she prepared. Dishes such as curry chicken back, brown stew chicken, or chicken back, rice and peas, boiled dumplings and banana, fried plantains, stew peas with salt pigtail or salt beef, ackee with fried smoke pig tripe, ackee with fried chicken back, ackee with salt fish, fish tea or fish soup, beef soup, run down with salt mackerel, run down with salt fish or fresh fish. There were so many more delicious Jamaican recipes.

When I was nine years old, my mother sent me to live with her eldest sister. I remember feeling very sad and abandoned. I missed my cousins and the freedom we had as children. My aunt was very strict and she did not allow me to have friends or to visit the neighbor's house. I was instructed to cook, wash clothes, and performed household chores at an early age. My aunt allowed me to read, write her letters, and complete applications for her. I remember the many times I wrote letters for her. Many of which were international letters to my aunt in England, my uncle in Cuba, and her sister-in-law in America.

I was told later that my aunt was not supposed to keep me. She had asked my mother for me to spend some time with her and to help her with letters during her recuperation from a major surgery, then my aunt refused to send me back home. I spent most of my childhood days thinking that my mother had sent me away and kept my other two younger siblings. I felt a sense of abandonment even though she and my stepfather visited me while I was living with my aunt. His name was Louis Chin. He was a very nice man. I remember his kindness to me to this very day. He was a manager at an insurance company in Ocho Rios, St. Ann. He would bring my mother to see me. They brought me money and other needed items.

My aunt instilled in me the value of education. I remembered her diligence with me all throughout elementary school. I had to come home and begin my school work right away. It was as if she was grooming me for things to come. I had no time to play with other children or go to the park. It was school, homework, and church. My aunt sent me to special teachers who helped me with homework, taught me to crochet, and knit. In the evenings after school, I sometimes went to Ms. Williams's house. Ms. William was my aunt's friend. She was very educated and talented. This lady was my very first mentor. We developed an unbreakable bond. I lived with my aunt from the age of nine until I was about 15 years old. Several events took place in my life while I was living with my aunt. Some were good memories and some were bad.

One of my most memorable experiences was finding a high school to attend after graduating from elementary school. I was very disappointed when I was told I passed the common entrance examination but was not given a spot in high school because they had no more space. That feeling haunted me for a long time. I drew closer to God when this happened. I remembered distinctly. The plan was for my family to send me to a private high school. The prerequisite was you had to pass the entrance examination. I took the examination and was waiting for the results. While waiting for the results, I visited my mother and the rest of the family in Little Bay. I found myself talking to God as I walked on the beach, bargaining with Him about my exam results. I told God, if he allowed me to pass this exam and gave me the opportunity to get into the school, I would serve him completely by becoming a preacher.

To my great joy, I passed the entrance examination and went on to attend the Continuation High School in HighGate, St. Mary. The school was managed by a religious organization known as the Friends-Quaker Church. That day, I kept my promise to God. I remain a believer to this day. I continued to attend the Emmanuel Baptist Church and learned more about God. As I attended, I had the privilege of being mentored by spiritual fathers and mothers. I became a part of the Emmanuel Youth Band. The members of the band were very close. We developed friendships that lasted even today. We performed in local and national events. As I attended

Sunday school and took Sunday school examinations at different levels, I was educated in the scriptures and even taught Sunday school from time to time. I participated in Baptist Church Summer Camp and Bible School. While attending church revival services, I met many notable ministers and crusade speakers, such as John and Andrew Gordon.

Chapter 3: My Teenage Years

I went back to live with my mother and the rest of my family when I was about 15 years old. The event that leads to me relocating back to the town of Little Bay was very stressful and will forever be imprinted in my memory. I thank God for his healing. I was young and really didn't understand how things happen or why sometimes no one really acknowledges what happens to young people. Sexual assault and abuse are real and wrong. For several years, I was sexually harassed.

It began with simple conversations to gain my confidence. Then there were subtle touches here and there. Yes touches; like touching me on the behind, or private part, or grabbing me as I passed by. The awkwardness of trying to play it off became uncomfortable because I did not know how to tell my aunt. I was in a good place and I was afraid to tell anyone. The man had a temper, he was mean, and he smoked marijuana. I did not know what he was going to do to me.

One morning my step-uncle and I were home alone. I was on my way to the bathroom when he tried to rape me. He grabbed at me like he normally does but this time it was different. He tried to put his hand up under my dress. I fought with anger to get him away from me. He was grabbing at me trying to hold me down as I fought. I found strength that I didn't realize I had. Before I knew it, I was running through the house and out of the back door to my neighbor's house. There we called my aunt and she came home. I told her what happened and she decided that I would stay with a teacher, who housed other children. My aunt did not want to send me home but she knew I wasn't safe in that environment.

When my mother heard about what happened she came to get me. I remember everyone being upset that day about what happened to me. But I dont remember anyone confronting my step-uncle about what he did. No one acknowledged what I went through. My experience of hurt, disappointment, and failure was suppressed subconsciously for many years. I grew up with feelings of inferiority and feeling unloved. I knew my family cared for me, but I felt unconnected to people.

I raised my kids and until they were older I was not able to express love to them. I love them and cared for them. But I knew something was wrong. Although I was married and had children, this experience held me in an emotional prison for years. When I met the

Prophets, they identified the hurt in me and they addressed it. They told me that God is healing the invisible gap that stood between my mother and me. They told me that God wants to heal me, but I was trying to heal myself. I felt that I had to take care of me by trusting no one but me. I was so wrong.

One day while my family and I were driving upstate, I was healed from the hurt of the past. I was all happy and unconcerned as I admired the beauty of the places we drove past. All of a sudden, my repressed vision came up vividly. I heard a voice saying very clearly, "You feel unloved, you were hurt, you experienced disappointment in the people you looked up to, they failed you, and they hurt you. Let it out. Look at the ugliness of this hurt. Don't repress it anymore. Let it go." I found myself crying and shaking for almost 15 minutes, as God healed me of my hurt. Everyone was asking me what was wrong, why I was crying? But I could not talk until it was over.

When it was all over, I felt so free and light. I felt the very love of God enfolding me in his arms. That day I was healed of the hurt of my past. I felt love and compassion flooding my being. The hatred, the inferiority, the abandonment, and feelings of hopelessness left me. When I returned to live with my mother, I remained connected to the Baptist Church and continued to attend school. My aunt would visit me bringing me items for school. I appreciated her care and concern. She has been a vital part of my growth and development. I thank God for her being in my life and I am present to the fact that she made me who I am today.

As I got older and learned more about the things of God, I began experiencing spiritual growth that leads me to become connected to a Christian group in my community. We were young Christian believers from various denominations, known as the Disciples for Christ. We were on fire for God and were invited to many church crusades and special events. Many souls came to Christ because of our ministry. We had the prison ministry, the hospital ministry, and open meetings in the town square.

I was a singer for the group. I would sing just before the preacher ministered the word of God. I would stand before the locked jail doors and minister to the prisoners, encouraging them to come to Jesus. Some of the most memorable experiences were feeling the anointing of God on my voice as I sang. It was as if I heard another voice singing. I was lost in the spirit of God as He anointed me. Some of the songs were: "Jesus is Still the Answer, Give Them All to Jesus, To God, Be the Glory, and Amazing Grace."

Chapter 4: From High School To College

When I graduated high school, I went to work at the Collector of Taxes in Kingston, Jamaica. I was later transferred to the Port Maria Collector of taxes office in St. Mary. There I saw Ms. Williams, who was my mentor when I was younger. She was in charge and my direct supervisor. I spent one year at the tax office. During that time, I developed a strong bond with several staff-members, developed skills, and experiences, which motivated me. To date, I maintain contact with them and I often visit the tax office whenever I am in Port Maria, St. Mary.

After I left the job at the tax office, I applied to the Nursing School at the University Hospital of the West Indies in Kingston. I was overjoyed with excitement when I was accepted. My family was so proud of this. I was the very first one in the family to do this. My paternal and maternal aunts and uncles in England bought my school books. My uncles and aunts in Jamaica helped me purchase uniforms, shoes, and other school supplies. I was so blessed that they all believed in me and helped me in my endeavors. I knew then I had to succeed. I was determined to make them proud.

I attended nursing school for three years. There I met and connected with some awesome women. We were called *Batch 84* because we were the 84th group to be trained in 1983. The experience was life changing. I had a spiritual mentor in the group. We attended church, concerts, and visited each during vacation. I went to Thompson Town in the parish of Clarendon for the very first time. I met her family, a wonderful group of people. There I learned to sing and to play the guitar. Today, I am a part of this wonderful family. My batch-mate is my second daughter's godmother.

We remain connected as sisters and have reunions every three years. Our children are everyone's "nieces and nephews." My youngest daughter came to our second reunion in Jamaica. We stayed at a resort in Ocho Rios. During the stay, my daughter and I had a small crisis. My batch mates were there to pray with us, to comfort, and encourage us. All was well because they made it well. They told her, "You are our niece."

Chapter 5: Migrating to the United State of America

After I graduated from nursing school, I worked in Jamaica for five years before migrating to the United States. I had no desire to come to the United States. My mind was changed one day when I experienced a so-called injustice with my house application. While working on my job, I was given the opportunity to contribute to the National Housing Trust (NHT). As a contributor, this agency allows you to apply for a loan to buy a house or land. I made an application and I was denied for a house loan. However, they gave me a loan to buy land. This was useless to me because I had no money to build a house on any land. I saw others getting houses, of which I presumed they had connections.

I was very disappointed in the system and felt betrayed as a contributor. So, when some USA recruiters came to recruit nurses for the healthcare institutions in the USA, I immediately applied for one of them. A male nurse and I were chosen for a Catholic hospital in New York. I was so excited and enthused. Later, I was so sad and disappointed when the US Embassy refused to give me the work Visa. They gave the male nurse his Visa but denied mine.

About a month or two later, new recruiters came to Jamaica recruiting for nursing programs. I went and applied. I was accepted for a major Jewish Hospital in the Bronx, New York. I was so excited until I learned that I could not apply for another Visa so soon. I asked a relative of my husband, who works in the embassy, is there anything that can be done on my behalf. She told me that was the rule and nothing can be done. I was sad and disappointed. I felt my dreams and my plans were falling apart. I heard of the great financial rewards and benefits of working in the health field in the USA. I was empowered and excited to help my husband and my two daughters migrate with me because I found out that they too could come with me to the USA with a special Visa.

After hearing the news, I went to the University of the West Indies hospital to visit my schoolmate who worked there. As I was walking on the campus, I met one of my church sisters, a student at the University. I decided to share my sad news with her. She looked at me and said "Dawn, man makes a rule, but God breaks them. So go and get your interview for your Visa." I felt encouraged by her words. My faith in God was strengthened and I felt empowered with faith.

I went to the embassy to put my application in by faith. Low and behold I saw one of the workers there that I know. She was my senior in high school. I told her about my problem and she immediately agreed to help me. That day she opened some doors for me that were closed. I was given an appointment and my work permit visa was approved. So God opened a door above all odds, and I was able to migrate to the USA, the land of great opportunity.

I worked at a wonderful medical center in the Bronx for over 12 years. While working in the Geriatric Unit, I met wonderful coworkers. These individuals are forever in my heart. Even today we keep in contact. Two of my coworkers are two of my daughters-godmother. My family and I were given our green cards after one year of working. I had to take the State Board exam and when I passed, we were able to apply for and obtain our Permanent Resident status. I had two more daughters who were born in the USA, which makes them automatic citizens. Later my husband, my other two daughters, and I became US citizens. I am forever grateful to this hospital for giving me the opportunity. Even today I feel much love and pride for this great institution as I see the great work it still performs throughout multiple towns in the state of New York.

During my early years of residency, our family was motivated to become foster parents. I was even more motivated because of my experiences as a child. I know what it is like not to have a father figure around and feel disconnected despite the motherly figures who mentored me. I felt motivated to take these children in and be a mother to them in the time when they were disconnected from their home and family. Foster parenting holds a special part in my heart. Despite some challenges and some drawbacks, our experience was overall very memorable and satisfying.

We loved and cared for multiple children over the years. We had small toddlers, teens, and even adults in our home. Our biological children bonded with many of our foster children. Even after we ceased from foster care, we still remained connected to some of the children. They have grown up into wonderful individuals, despite their challenges. Some of our foster children found us on Facebook and remain connected to us.

Dawn presenting her project at the Sigma Theta Tau International Honor Society of Nursing 30th Nursing Research Congress in Calgary, Canada (2019)

Dawn's Mother-Joycelyn Gordon-Danvers

Owen Silvera (on the right) and Leon Silvera (on the left), *The Legendary Silvera Brothers* (Jamaican Ska Artists in the 1960s). Dawn received a prophetic word about, "The family legacy-gift of music- was handed down to the family." Dawn and her daughters did inherit the gift of music.

Daughters: Velicia, Nickeisha, Crystal & Destini

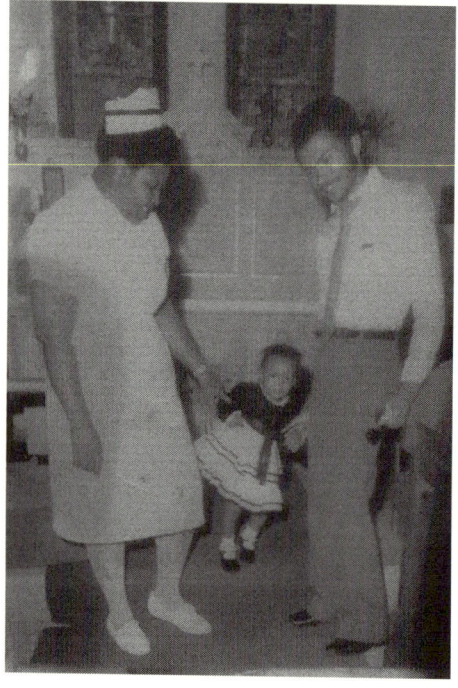

Dawn, Lenworth Bardowell, and Velicia

First Grandchild-Kairo Green, son of Velicia and Ashaney Green.

Born on 7/15/2020

Velicia and her husband Ashaney Green

Brother Norman Rose, wife Sophia Rose and son Sanjay Rose

Dawn's niece Charlene Rose & son Taquan Henry

Dawn, with Charlene, and Sanjay (niece and nephew)

Sharlon, Amanda, Angelina, Aiden

Debby, Nihal, and Nickeal (Dawn's sister and nieces)

Dawn's Sister-Paula Campbell with her late husband Carlton Campbell
(Bampy)

Dawn's sister Marcia & niece Marissa

Dawn, Mother Joyce, daughters, nieces, nephews

Dawn, cousin Cardina, and her late Aunt Audrey,
affectionately known as (Aunty Biggest)

Aunt Eulalee Ricketts with one of her neighbors
(Jamaica)

Dawn and Giran Ndure

Dr. Dawn Silvera-Ndure, Aunt Florence Hinds, cousin Trecia & daughter at
Graduation in Florida (2017)

Dawn been anointed to the role of Deacon by Arch Bishop Bernard Jordan
of Zoe Ministries Church of New York (2018)

Dawn and volunteers participating in the Friends of Port Maria, New York Chapter Inc. Medical Mission at the Mason Hall Anglican Church in St. Mary, Jamaica West

Dawn and Volunteer participating in the Friends of Port Maria, New York Chapter Inc. Medical Mission at the Emmanuel Baptist Church in Port Mari, (2016)

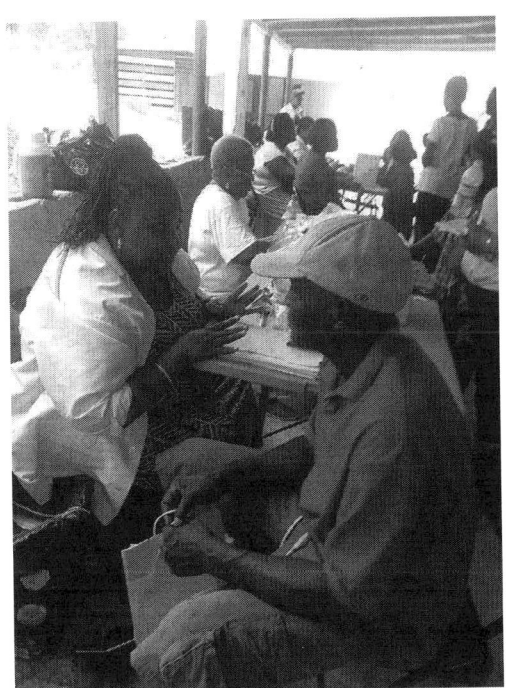

Dawn and Volunteers who participated in the Friends of Port Maria, New York Chapter Inc. Medical Mission at the Preston Hill Roman Catholic Church (Jamaica)

Dawn and Volunteers (2016) who participated in the Friends of Port Maria, New York Chapter Inc. Medical Mission at the Galina Church of Christ, West Indies

Chapter 6: Prophetic Manifestations

Before I came to Zoe Ministries in 1996, I had no knowledge of the prophetic ministry or of a modern-day prophet. My experience in my culture was limited to those we called "reader woman "or "reader man," gifted people in our culture who were sought after for spiritual guidance or for help to remove curses. Some were referred to as "obeah woman" or "obeah man," who put a curse on a person and or remove a curse. Many went to see these individuals in secret. They were paid for their services.

When I was in high school, I was taken to see a spiritual healer, known as a reader woman. She was also called "mother" and was gifted in spiritual vision, healing, and removal of curses. I was having terrible headaches that would not go away. I was told that my close friend and classmate's grandmother placed a curse on me because I was very bright and I would always come in first place in my class exams. The mother told my family that she gave me a pencil that was used to steal my destiny. The mother gave me a bottle of "tonic" to drink. To my amazement, the headaches were gone. I was supposed to follow up for a second bottle of the drink but did not go back. The weird headaches never came back.

The Prophetic Dreamer

I started dreaming about dreams that came to pass just. I never understood my role as a dreamer until I connected with the ministry of the Master Prophet, E. Bernard Jordan. I became intrigued with the process of prophetic dreaming. I considered doing research on this topic on an international level. I even spoke to my co-workers from different cultures and countries and was stunned by the similarities of their dream state. In my dream, I saw information on situations happening on a national and international level. The dreams also concerned current situations in the media or things to come. I always tell my family about each dream that stands out and document each dream. I did not understand why I started to dream things that came to pass. I ignored it and pondered in my heart. Here are some of my dreams.

Dreams with Revelations

This dream occurred in Jamaica when I was in my 20's just as I graduated from nursing school. I went to work in a community hospital in the town where I was born. One night, I saw the surgeon in my dream. He was lying on a stretcher with green operating sheets around him. I went to work the next day and found out thieves robbed him and shot him. He required suturing of his wounds. So he was taken to the operating room for the procedure.

Several years later, I came to the US and my young cousin passed. Not long after I had several dreams of him in wandering situations, like floating in the sea, wandering aimlessly about. I never understood what was happening. In one dream, I saw myself taking him across a large green field with beautiful green grass. As I came to a door, I was about to take him inside and then I heard a voice say, "It is his time to go in, it's not your time."

My cousin went inside and I never saw him in my dream again until many years later, when his daughter migrated to the US. That dream was made clear to me when I came to the house of the Prophets. I then understood that I was helping my cousin to find his way over the other side. He was able to find rest and wondered no more.

Dream Manifestation

I remembered vividly my dreams of the presidential election several years ago. The Republican presidential candidate came to me in my dream. It was as if I was watching a movie. He was dressed in a nice suit and he stood in an office. He looked very happy. I knew in the dream that he was the president of the United States. That same week after my dream, the said candidate is declared the winner of the election and the president of the USA.

Many years ago, there was a very famous murder trial in the media. It involved a prominent African-American sports figure. A few days before the verdict, he appeared in my dream and spoke to me about the outcome of the trial. He told me that he was acquitted. Just like I dreamt it, they found him not guilty and he was acquitted.

Dream Manifestation

On March 30, 2011, I had a frightening dream. In this dream, I saw a large round grey-colored stone fall in the sea. At that same time, I saw a piece of grey color stone pointing upwards in the sea. The pointed stone was next to the spot where the round stone fell. I immediately felt fear and the sense of the water rising under my feet. Just then, I felt the earth shake under my feet. I looked and saw a great wave of water rising upwards towards the sky. This great wave of water then fell and started to flow towards the land. I heard people crying as I felt water flowing around us. I woke up at that point. A few months after the dream, great flooding took place in different states in the US.

Dream Manifestation

My prophetic dream on April 19, 2011 was about me in my church having a meeting. The meeting was held in a hotel conference room. Me and another person were on our way to the hotel in a vehicle. As I drove along the road, I passed a large open field on my right. In this field, I saw a large tent. I saw people walking towards the tent on their way to the meeting. I said to myself that it is a very good location. People will see and come to visit as they pass by. Immediately after that scene, I was in a building. As we entered the building, we were confronted by a group of men who were dressed in strange-looking robes. These men looked like native Indians or Aramaic dressed in their traditional clothing. They had weapons in their hands that looked like bows and arrows and other ancient-looking weapons. Others came to join them. We started to run as they surrounded us.

I felt a sense of fear as we attempted to run away from them. Immediately after, I felt a sense of peace and feelings of danger lifted. After that scene, we found ourselves inside the tent. The group of men, who were chasing us, followed us inside the tent. Immediately as they came in, I felt the notion that they wanted us to teach them what we knew. They wanted us to teach them about the Creator and his awesome ways. The dream ended in the tent as they all came in. As time went on, I learned to ask God for the interpretation of my dreams and how to process them in the natural, what it means, and how I should pray.

Chapter 7: What is Prophecy?

Webster states, "prophecy is the foretelling or prediction of what is to come; something that is declared by a prophet, especially a divinely inspired prediction, instruction, or exhortation; a divinely inspired utterance or revelation: oracular prophecies" (*Webster* 2017). The gift of prophecy edifies, exhorts, and comforts; helps us build up or strengthen; and should lead us to the word of God (I Corinthians 14:3). Prophecy "involves a process in which one or more messages are allegedly communicated by God. Such messages typically involve inspiration, interpretation, or revelation of divine will concerning the prophet's social world and events to come" (compared to divine knowledge) (*Webster* 2003). Prophecy is not limited to any one culture. Below are some prophetic words I received over the years and their fulfillment.

A House Miracle

In 2008 while renting, I decided to buy a house. While waiting for the closing to take place, I suddenly discovered the house I rented was foreclosed on and my landlord never told me. We were instructed to move out. I went to the court and asked the judge for time. He did the best he could, but could not guarantee the extra time. I was hoping to move into my new house before being evicted. No one knew our dilemma, but God did. I went to church one day and the Lord spoke to my situation. Prophet Manasseh said, "God is working out the housing situation; you will not rent, you will own."

The day before the sheriff was scheduled to come, God moved on my behalf and the bank gave us a closing date. The problem was solved. My daughter and I were afraid to drive the moving van, so God sent us someone to drive for us for a good price. We rented a *U-Haul* truck and packed our furniture and belongings. We then parked the truck on the street nearby. The night before the sheriff came, my four daughters, our dog Prince, and I checked into a hotel nearby. The next morning the sheriff came and we gave him the keys to the empty house. Later that day, we went to our house closing and received the keys to our own house. God is truly amazing. That is the Power of Prophecy.

The Legacy of Music

Many years ago the prophet told me these words, "The family legacy will be handed down to you." I pondered on the meaning of those words. I knew there were no rich family members that I knew of; that would leave me an inheritance. As the years passed, I saw the prophecy fulfilled before my very eyes. It was not an inheritance "legacy" but it was "artistic gifting." *The Silvera Brothers* songs are still being played in Jamaica and Europe even today. I made a *Facebook* page in honor of the group. So far hundreds of people from Europe, Latin America and Jamaica have come to his page and express their love for the group. My father once told me that he was in the studio with famous Jamaican artists like Bob Marley, Dennis Brown, Denny Morgan, and Beres Hammond.

Each of my daughters is gifted in the arts. They write poems, songs, act, paint, sing, or draw. When they were younger, they sang together in a group at church functions. Their favorite songs were those of Elvis Presley and Michael Jackson. Crystal and Nickeisha have embraced the gift of singing more than the other two. Velicia and Destini have many talents but they choose to focus on writing poems and stories. One of my daughters plays a musical instrument and has won many awards. She is presently working on developing her musical skills. To date she has written hundreds of songs. In addition, she had recorded and produced many of these songs at home. The legacy handed down to me is manifesting just as the word of the Lord was spoken.

Destiny Restored

I received prophetic words from the Master Prophet, E. Bernard Jordan. He stated, "God has given you a great mind. You can do anything." This prophecy came to me many years ago when I doubted my ability to enroll in graduate study. I never told anyone about my fears. When I was a teenager in Jamaica, someone who was influential in my life killed my dream of becoming a doctor so I thought. They told me "Don't study too hard, people who study hard get sick in their head. Just do something that you can manage." The person meant well, but they really discouraged me. This was why I feared the idea of graduate studies. The prophet came in my life and pushed me to my destiny. I was able to believe his word and overcome my fears.

I was a nurse when I decided that I wanted to enroll in Medical school and become a doctor. I applied and was accepted into the Columbia University Post Baccalaureate Pre-Med program, in Manhattan. All my family, friends, and my church family were all so excited and elated for me. This was my dream and the start of my journey to become a medical doctor. God showed me that day that if I truly wanted it he was willing to give it to me. He showed me that all things are possible if I believe his Prophet. I started my journey by doing Advanced Calculus courses. I was scheduled to do several electives before the actual medical courses. Eventually, I decided to divert my plans, because I felt the basic courses would take me a while.

That's when God showed me a shorter route. I then decided that I wanted to become a Family Nurse Practitioner (FNP). The FNP is a medical provider, who performs the work of a medical doctor in every capacity. I was accepted to a graduate nursing program in Riverdale, New York. More than half way through the program, the Nursing Tutor failed my colleague and I during one of our practical exam. She stated "you both ran out of time" This was a shock to many of our other collegues. We were not allowed back into the program, despite appealing to the college school board. The college never gave us another chance. Many people encouraged to take them to court, but we did not. I eventually I transferred to Lehman's college in the Bronx, New York. The college did not offer the FNP program at that time, so I completed my Masters Degree in Nursing as a Clinical Nurse Specialist.

The plan was to eventually complete my degree as a FNP at a later time in another college. I kept delaying it for a while. While I was working as a Nursing Supervisor in a Nursing Home, I was motivated by a male nurse to complete my studies to become a Nurse Practitioner. I will forever be grateful to Nurse Douglas Cherry for motivating me to be a Family Nurse Practitioner. Each night he comes on duty, he comes into the nursing office and said "You don't belong here in this nursing office" I finally listened to him and promised him that I will apply to a nursing college.

I then applied and was accepted into the Graduate Nursing Degree Program at Pace University in Pleasantville, New York. There I obtained a post graduate degree as a Family Nurse Practitioner. When Nurse Cherry passed away in 2019, I attended his home going service in Mount Vernon, New York. In appreciation for his influence in my life and my career, I performed Andre Crouch's inspirational song "My Tribute-How can I say Thanks" I will be forever grateful to this dedicated nurse who God used to pushed me into my destiny.

The Prophet does speak even in one's examination challenges. I remembered my FNP certification was very challenging. I was not able to pass it at my first attempts. Then one day, I decided to ask the

Master Prophet, Bishop Bernard Jordan for guidance. He told me to take the exam on September 16th that year. I took my exam that very same day and I passed it. God still speaks today, through his Prophets

Miracle Car

Couple years ago, I bought a car that was appropriate for then. I was only able to get a vehicle at a high interest rate. Then I decided to upgrade but I could not get anyone to approve me because I still owed a lot of money on my vehicle. I keep hearing many prophecies about a new car but I just never went because they never approved me. December 2016, I was in church and service was almost over when a prophetess took the microphone and called out my name and said "Prophetess Dawn go and get that car, go and get that car you need, God said go and get it". Something in me vibrated with that word and I felt motivated to go and get the car. I went to a known dealer who would not approve me because I owed too much on my vehicle. I believed the Prophet, so I did not give up at the first try. I went to a second dealer and the dealer approved me. That day, I received many favors and discounts. My interest was a lot lower than my previous loan. I found favor with the dealer, the loan officer, and the general manager that day. My daughters were with me and we all got into the most beautiful truck that day.

Oral Presentation Miracle

I remembered with gratitude how Prophet Levar Samuels from Florida was instrumental in praying for my breakthrough at the final journey towards graduating with my doctorate degree. I started graduate school in fall of 2013. I completed my main classes then waited for my Doctorate in Nursing Practice (DNP) project approval. As I was nearing the end of my long journey, things started to get very weird. My final paper was misplaced. Then when I received a response, the program was changed. I had to rewrite my project into the new format. After that I waited and waited for approval until I became so stressed I ended up in the hospital with chest pressure. God saved my life that day. Prior to my admission in the hospital, the prophets came to me during prophetic conferences and prayed for my chest area. I had no symptoms other than signs of stress. One prophet told me, "God is healing your heart. All is well." That day of my hospitalization, I did several tests for the heart. As just like the prophet said, my heart was functioning well.

During the long wait, I received encouraging words from other prophets. Not many people knew I was waiting for my doctoral degree to be conferred. So when I hear words like "I see you with a doctor in front of your name," I knew that was the work of God. As I waited, I was encouraged by the prophetic word I received from one of our ministers, Prophet Devon Thompson, who made his transition to be with the Lord. Even when I was not yet in the doctorate program, he said to me, "I see you in school, you will have a doctor in front of your name." While feeling discouraged for waiting so long for my oral presentation appointment, I decided to ask my friend Prophet Samuel for prayer. He prayed and spoke positive words into my life. That very week, I received words of my appointment for the oral presentation. I was excited because once I pass this presentation my work is ready to be sent to the Dean's Office for final editing and approval. One miracle after another happened.

During the oral presentation, my professors asked each other if they had any recommendation. To my amazement and joy, each professor said they approved my presentation. Thanks to God, in November 2016 my degree was conferred. I was so excited. I could not wait for the summer 2017 graduation in Maryland. I decided to go for the January 6, 2017 graduation in Florida. My aunt Florence came in from Brooklyn and my two cousins from Florida were present to support me. My aunt, Florence, is my youngest aunt. She has been a tower of strength to me over the years. She attended all my graduations. Although my daughters, my husband, and the rest of family could not make it, they were overjoyed at my good news and supported me emotionally and financially for the graduation.

A Step into A New Future

I was married to the father of my daughters for approximately 30 years. We were separated in 2000, because of various indifferences and failures on both sides. We both made mistakes and we both played a significant part in causing the marriage to fail. I remember we were young and in love in the country of Jamaica. We both were from different denominational, and educational backgrounds, but we connected with our love for Christ and the things of God. We went through many barriers and struggles in our relationship and got married despite the fight. We stayed married for many years and attended church together. We served the Lord in sincerity. When we separated, I tried on many occasions to repair the marriage. Sadly, it never happened. Even when we were living in the house with our family, we were separated emotionally and socially. Today, I looked back and I acknowledged my part in causing this separation. I have now made peace with myself and with my ex-husband. Today, we communicate and have a good relationship. Over those years, he has been a good father to our daughters and to the foster children we took care of for more than six years.

Chapter 8: Two Cultures Became One

I remained single for many years. I was always in school, so I focused on my job and my education. I realized as the time approached for me to complete my FNP Degree, it was not healthy for me to be alone. I started to attend events, such as karaoke, concerts, reggae shows, and so on but I realized the types of men hitting on me in these environments were not compatible with me. So, I eventually stopped going.

In 2005, we relocated from the Bronx to a prominent town in the Westchester area of New York. In 2008, we purchased a house and moved to an address nearer to the town square. We usually shop at the variety store in the town square. Each time I shop at the store, I was instantly drawn to the tall, dark, and handsome undercover security guard at the store. I even said to my older daughter, "He is cute, don't you think." Each time I came he would strike up a conversation with me and we eventually got along okay.

We went at this for about two years. I never knew he was interested in me until one Halloween day he came up to me and asked me out. He gave me his number just in time because that weekend I was invited by friends to attend a famous annual singles retreat. I had a trip planned and paid for, so I still attended. I never showed any interest in dating anyone I met there. I performed at the karaoke sessions, attended the live concert with entertainment, and enjoyed the great food.

When I returned home, I was invited on my first date. I was feeling so blessed and happy. After several dates, I realized that I was falling in love. I was still not won over because I knew we were from two different backgrounds. He was from Gambia in West Africa and he was from the Muslim faith. To make matters even more interesting, he was younger than me.

I was at a crossroad, not knowing what to do. He expressed how much he loved me and wanted to marry me. I told him no. He was very disappointed. He told me that he has many family members who were Christians. He told that his sister is a diplomat who brought him, his mother, and his younger brother to the United States. He and his brother stayed in the US, but his sister and mother reside in Rome, Italy. His sister works for the United Nations. He introduced me to them as we spoke via telephone. He had other siblings and family members living in Gambia and other parts of

Europe. Despite knowing his family and realizing his legitimate background, I was still hesitant in marrying him.

One day while I was attending a prophetic conference, I received clear and precise prophetic words by a young prophetess. She was blindfolded and never saw my face. She said to me, "why are you drawing away from him, he has tried and tried and you are running from him." She encouraged me to accept him. The prophetic word left me speechless. I said to myself that not many people knew I was separated. So why am I getting this word? That day, I decided to get a divorce and accept the marriage proposal. My sister-in-law came from Italy with her daughter and other family members. My brother-in-law came from the Bronx and each accepted me as a part of the family. I attempted to have a Christian minister perform the wedding, but they refused. I was very disappointed with them. I was afraid to tell my Bishop about my wedding.

Eventually, I told him about the wedding and invited several members to attend. They came to support me and Bishop Jordan sent one of the ministers to help us with the program. It was a beautiful experience, which I will never forget. I was very reluctant to go to my church after my marriage. When I finally attended church, I was so surprised and overjoyed at the response I received from the members. Bishop Jordan greeted me warmly, putting his arms around me congratulating me. The favor of God was with our marriage from the start. Like many, during the early period of the marriage, we both were confronted with differences in culture, values, and personality. I received many prophetic words that encouraged me not to give up. One day, I was at another prophetic conference and Prophet Manasseh called me out and said, "God said don't walk away from your marriage, stay in your marriage."

My journey is filled with many instances of prophetic words related to our union. One day a visiting prophet from Africa called me out in the service. He also called out my full name, birthplace, and my husband's name, birthplace and religion. He further went on to tell me about some family issues connected to his family in Gambia, West Africa. The prophet then told me about my life as a young teen and mentioned certain painful incidents that occurred. He further encouraged me to go forward towards greatness. My Bishop was amazed because not many people at church knew that my husband was of the Muslin faith.

Recently as in the last two years, I was confronted with challenges from individuals who were instrumental in attempting to bring division and doubts in our union. God sent a young prophet from Florida who was praying for us and encouraging me throughout the trials and challenges. In the end, the enemy was defeated and the father opened doors of favor for us. God granted us the desires of our heart and favor found us as we obtained our new home. Not only was this place priced at the exact price we were praying for, it was also very near my children and the rest of the family.

Chapter 9: Emotional Healing

On November 9, 2018, God healed my heart from a chronic issue that was eating at me over the years. God addressed questions that plagued me for years in regards to my feelings of missing out on the mother-daughter bond with my children as they grew up. I felt as if I did not connect emotionally with my children when they were growing up. Somehow, I became cognitive that when they reached the age of five, feelings of separation came between us and I did not understand why. I questioned it for years and eventually, I let it slip by.

On the morning of November 9, 2018, I was dropping my daughter, Velicia, off at work. As we drove along, she told me she was not feeling well. I acknowledged her complaint from a medical perspective as I usually do and then dropped her off at her destination. As I drove off, I suddenly felt a feeling of sadness and guilt overwhelming me. As these feelings tore at my inside, I knew then that God was speaking to me and was about to bring healing to my situation. Immediately, I called my daughter on her phone and began to encourage her as a mother.

I felt a great wave of motherly love crashing down on me. I told her to take care of herself and to feel better. I told her I love her as a mother. I actually felt like a mother talking to her daughter. I started to cry as I was driving to work. The spirit of God spoke to me. At that moment God showed me the situation that confronted me when they were growing up. He allowed me to see why I felt a sense of separation between myself and when they reached the age of five. God removed the curse from me. That day, He healed my heart from feeling separated and being separated from my mother that plagued me for years.

God allowed me to understand why I felt that way. That's the age I experienced feelings of abandonment. There are many occasions in which God delivered me from psychological issues that bothered me for years. Out of the blue, he would bring up psychological issues that lie dormant in my subconscious. Then he performs a complete restoration and heals me from the hurt of my past. God is faithful, even when we do not realize we need him.

Chapter 10: God Answers the Seed

While I was writing the book in January 2019, I recalled other testimonies of the goodness of God towards me. In 2018, I experienced financial setbacks connected to non-payments from a tenant. Eventually, I ended up in foreclosure court for several months. During this time, I continued in faith as I attended each hearing accompanied by my counselor from a non-profit agency. I experienced several months of restless sleep and worrisome days. But God my heavenly Father, kept me through it all. He opened doors for me to obtain added income. I found a new rental income by hosting local and international guests. In addition, I found a part-time job that was very convenient for me to do two to three times a week. This job was for a couple of hours in the evening after my regular job. God continued to bless me with favor and increase.

During the *Harvest Revival* of November 2018 at my church, Zoë Ministries, I sowed a seed to assist our Bishop E. Bernard Jordan and the Company of Prophets to visit Swaziland. The King of Swaziland requested our Archbishop to come to Swaziland to bless and anoint the New President of Swaziland. Two-events unfolded after I sowed the seed. The first event was connected to my cousin's daughter. My cousin called me with some disturbing news. She told me that her daughter found a lump in her breast in July 2018. They both spoke to me as I tried to gather the severity of the situation. One doctor told her to have the surgery. Another doctor wanted to do chemotherapy and radiation therapy. I advised her not to do any surgery until the biopsy was complete. She promised to send me the biopsy report. I spoke encouraging words to their spirit and told them to have faith in God. I cried and cried as I hung up the phone.

I did not know who to talk to. I decided not to spread any negative vibes, so I called my church sister and asked for her prayer. I pondered on it. I said God, she is so young and a hardworking young girl. Please save her. I poured out my heart in prayer for her as I sat in my car after leaving work. I attempted to tell my daughter and then stopped. I went home and later that night lo and behold, the Master Prophet E. Bernard Jordan called me on my cell phone. He gave me several prophecies about my daughters and their father. He said their father was facing a health challenge. But God will see him through. He then said, "Someone on my mother's side of the family was facing some health challenge." I immediately told him about my cousin. He prophesied health and healing for her and told me to tell her that God will see her through and that all is well. I was so elated to see God moving on my cousin's behalf. I texted her and told her, God's got your back, keep believing. You are coming through.

Chapter 11: My 12 Gripping Giants Will Fall

This chapter tells of the second event that occurred because of the seed. On December 31, 2018, I attended the New Year Eve service at church. The message was centered on identifying the "Twelve Gripping Giants" in our lives and to write them down on paper. These giants represent twelve challenging problems we were facing in our lives. We received a prophetic stone from the Master Prophet that will hold a message for us on conquering these giants in our lives. My giants were identified and I wrote them down as instructed. As I went to sow my seeds, I received a word from the Master Prophet, E. Bernard Jordan. He prophesied to me about the very first giant I wrote down. He told me that God was about to deliver an individual who was close to me, from an addiction problem. I marveled at the work of God. That night he addressed a matter that was tearing at my heart for over 10 years. I held up my hand to God and I praised him for the word I heard. I took my stone from the hand of the Master Prophet E. Bernard Jordan and the word written on the stone was "Victory. "

The problem of alcohol addiction is real to many families who face the effects. This family member did not accept that he was addicted. If he did, he never admitted it to me or listened to my suggestion for him to seek help at a rehab center. Each day he came home from work he had severe mood changes, delusions, memory loss, anxiety episodes, and some aggressive moods. Several times during these mood changes and aggressive behavior, I called the EMT to take him to the hospital. When they came, they stated that he refused help, so they could not force him. I finally gave up and never called them again.

I reached out to other family members for help. They just sympathize. No one reached out to motivate or confront him to seek medical help. One family member stated that he spoke to him and he seemed ok to them. That was because he deceived him during the conversation. He is a master manipulator, who lies his way during any conversation that confronts his alcoholism. There is complete denial, paranoia, expressions of "self-righteousness" and loss of apathy for his behavior. It has been a journey dealing with this person. Someone told me that this is my cross and my trial. Even as I write this chapter, I see the situation each day. Sometimes I feel like abandoning the individual and taking them off my caring list, but God said his grace is sufficient for me. So I walk on in faith and believe the word the Prophets have given to me over the years.

Chapter 11: He is an On-time God

I am a member of the Sigma Theta Tau International Honor Society of Nursing for 10 years, but I never attended a Sigma Conference until an opportunity presented itself. The membership was given to me while I attend college for nursing as I maintain a required GPA in my studies. Each inductee remains a member after graduation. Sigma nurses are found in all cultures. Later, I found out that Sigma members consist of students, graduate nurses, and professors. I was invited to submit an Abstract for the 30th Annual Nursing Research Conference in July 2019, in Alberta Canada. I decided to submit my Abstract from my DNP project. To my surprise, it was accepted. I was excited about participating in the conference. In addition to this, I was working on my $1000 conference fee, obtaining my ticket, and my hotel. The financial responsibility began to create doubt in attending the conference.

I attended the Prophetic Conference in Mexico in February 2019. During one of our daily sessions, a guest speaker was teaching. His teaching was a spiritual eye-opener for me. He spoke clearly and directly as if he was talking to me. He said, "God wants to make your name great" it was as if God was saying to me I want to showcase your talents and gifts. I want to do things for you in your profession as you connect with your peers." My eyes were opened as God spoke to my heart. I decided there and then that I will find the money and I would register for the conference.

As I attended the conference in July 2019 in Canada, I was amazed and excited to see hundreds of nurses from all over the world. There were nurses from every area of the nursing profession, university professors, researchers, Nurse Practitioners, Specialty nurses, and student nurses. During opening night, I was sitting in a room with women and men who possess great minds. Some individuals with PhDs, Doctor in Nursing Science Doctorate in Nursing Practice, Master's and Bachelor degrees. I never knew that this research conference was going on for so many years and that it was held in the various countries of the world. I was fortunate to be attending the 30th Annual Nursing Research Conference.

I learned so much at this conference. I know God wanted me to be there. I met honorees from various disciplines whose research was inducted in the hall of fame. As these honorees presented their topics and projects, I learned so much. I became present to the fact that the nursing profession has individuals with brilliant minds. I met several nurses from Jamaica, South Africa, and Bermuda, who I connected with and we became friends. I also met a nurse who graduated several years before me, from my nursing school in Jamaica. I was so happy to see someone from my own nursing school. While attending the conference, I became present to the fact that it is a very fortunate experience when ones' Abstract was accepted at the research conference. I met a nurse from Jamaica, who lives in Florida. She was surprised to see that I was attending for the first time and that I was a presenter.

Even as I document more prophetic breakthroughs and fulfillment in the year 2019, I am drawn to recent events that strengthen my faith in God. I recall, the gas company came to my house to replace gas meters and discovered a small leak. My gas system was turned off. The plumber came and estimated that we needed to pay $4000 to fix the system and get back heat and hot water. I was faced with a challenge on how to pay for a new gas meter. I had just returned from Jamaica, travel expenses, and helping with my aunt's funeral expenses. That week I was at church and was listening to a message from a visiting Bishop Jordan. This message helped to unlock the resources that helped me obtain funds to pay for the heating system. The message was based on the Prophet Elisha and the miracle of the widow's oil. The Bishop gave us a powerful message on "Use what is in your house." That very week God showed me what was in my house. I obtained the $4000 from my daughters, my son-in-law, and other sources.

While I was facing a financial challenge, I dealt with some emotional challenges and family issues. In the past, I have proven that God always comes through for me when I stay focused on him and on his work. He always comes through in my darkest hour or impossible situation. He always sends me messages of comfort and inspires me to take my eyes off my problems and to focus on him. I decided to make one-to-one calls for the ministry. I know from past experiences, when I take care of God's business he always takes care of mine.

After ministering to a partner and telling her that God will part the Red Sea on her behalf, I told her that God said to tell her He breaks policies and rules on her behalf and gives her the victory in her situation. She started to cry and was praising God. For she knew what she was going through. I did not know, but God knew. Immediately after completing the call and hanging up the phone, my car radio that was on the K-Love station started playing a song titled, "He will carry you." The Lord spoke to me through the song. The words are, "There is no problem too great that God cannot solve it. No mountain too tall that he cannot move it. There is no storm too dark God cannot calm it. There is no sorrow too deep He cannot soothe it. If he carried the weight of the world upon his shoulder, I know my brother that he will carry you. If he carried the weight of the world upon his shoulder, I know my sister He will carry you" written by Scott Wesley Brown.

Chapter 12: Healing and Faith

I rest in the assurance that God is my all in all. Are you faced with life stressors, do you require physical or psychological healing? The father calls out to us in Matthew 11: 28-30 (NKJV) and says, "Come unto me, all ye that labor and are heavy laden, and I will give you rest. Take my yoke upon you, and learn of me; for I am meek and lowly in heart: and ye shall find rest unto your souls. For my yoke is easy, and my burden is light." Our God is a Healer. The Hebrew word Raphe means "heal, restore, or make whole." In Exodus 15, shortly after His own people left Egypt for the Promised Land, God revealed himself to them as Yahweh Rophe, "the God who heals" or "God is your healer."

Exodus 15: 26 (NKJV) says, "If thou wilt diligently hearken to the voice of the LORD thy God, and wilt do that which is right in his sight, and wilt give ear to his commandments and keep all His statutes, I will put none of these diseases upon thee, which I have brought upon the Egyptians: For I am the Lord that heals thee."

In Genesis 1: 1-6, the word of God reads, "In the beginning, God created the heavens and the earth. The earth was without form and void, and darkness was over the face of the deep. And the Spirit of God was hovering over the face of the waters. And God said, let there be light, and there was light. And God saw that the light was good. And God separated the light from the darkness. God called the light Day, and the darkness he called Night. And there was evening and there was morning, the first day (NKJV)."

God created a new life where there is no darkness. He is willing and ready to heal that which is out of alignment in your body. Are you willing to remove the band aid off the wound and let him perform a surgical restoration that heals? As the songwriter says, "a brand new experience can be yours as "you arise and be healed in the name of Jesus."

Bibliography

Holy Bible: The New King James Version, containing the Old and New Testaments. (1982). Nashville: T. Nelson.

Merriam-Webster's Collegiate Dictionary, (Eleventh Edition.), (2003), Springfield, Mass: Merriam-Webster, Inc.

Silvera-Ndure, D. (2016), *"Development of a Church-Based Educational Program to Increase Prostate Cancer Screening for Black Men 40 and Older" Walden Dissertations and Doctoral Studies Collection* at _ScholarWorks@waldenu.edu_.

About Dr. Dawn Silvera-Ndure, FNP

Dr. Dawn Silvera–Ndure is a Family Nurse Practitioner, board certified by the American Association of Nurse Practitioners (AANP) and currently licensed to practice in New York State. Dr. Dawn Silvera-Ndure, is married to Giran Ndure and is the mother of four beautiful daughters and a new born grandson Dr. Dawn Silvera-Ndure loves to sing, and write songs. She performs for friends, family, co-workers and churches at special events.

She began her training in nursing in 1983 at the University Hospital of the West Indies in Kingston Jamaica. Dawn became a Registered Nurse and has been working in the nursing profession for over 37 years. In 1983- She graduated from the UWI school of nursing in Jamaica with a Diploma in nursing. She was employed by the Ministry of Health and worked for several years, in her home town at the Port Maria Hospital in St. Mary. Dawn was later transferred to the St. Ann's Bay Hospital. During this time, Dawn worked in the Emergency room, the medical/surgical unit, the pediatric unit, and the operating room.

In 1989 Dawn migrated to the United States of America, after been recruited by Montefiore Medical Center in Bronx New York. Dawn worked on the medical/ surgical unit, the emergency room and the geriatric unit at Montefiore Medical Center. In 2003, Dawn went to work for the Jewish Guild for the Blind Nursing Home in Yonkers New York, as a Nursing Supervisor. Dawn was transferred to the Jewish Guild for the Blind Home Care Agency in Manhattan. Here she worked as a Nurse Case Manager. In this role she, developed and implemented care plans for members in the community; Evaluated the status of the member's physical, social and environmental conditions; Collaborated with members, providers, consultants as well as family members;

Supervised team members and consultants in performing assigned tasks; and Conducted physical, psycho-social and environmental assessments for the clients in their home

In 2009, Dawn went to work for the St. Cabrini Nursing Home as an Administrative Nursing Coordinator. In 2011, after completing her Family Nurse Practitioner (FNP) degree, Dawn entered the field of community Home Health Care and obtained her first FNP job as a contractual Nurse Practitioner at NP in Family Health-Gericine Solution, in New York. In this role she: Provided home visits in the Tri-State Area doing in home assessments, hospital visits, treatment and monitoring of clients with mental health issues. She also did home visit for patients with chronic medical conditions, diagnosing and treating chronic diseases, doing physical examinations, monitoring, educating and counseling patients, collaborating and referring to other providers. In 2014, Dawn obtained a full time job at the Mount Vernon Neighborhood Health Center Inc. Mount Vernon, New York. Here she and a Medical Assistance was sent to open and operate a brand new school based health center, at the Mount Vernon High School. Dawn presently works at the MVNHC community clinic and their School Based Health Center.

Publication

In 2016, Dawn completed her studies at Walden University and obtained her Doctorate in Nursing Practice Degree (DNP). Her doctoral project was: *Development of a Church-Based Educational Program to Increase Prostate Cancer Screening for Black Men 40 and Older.* The goal of the project was to develop an evidence-based, theory-supported education and referral program to promote prostate cancer prevention screening among African-American men utilizing New York Community church settings. The resultant scholarly project aims to motivate the target population towards prostate cancer prevention screening as appropriate through the development of an evidence-based, theory-supported, community-focused education and referral program using self-efficacy theory.

This project provides a program, grounded in self-efficacy, that will educate African-American men about prostate cancer, empower them with knowledge regarding risk, motivate them to seek preventative screenings, and obtain care if needed. An evaluation strategy was developed incorporating a post-test questionnaire to measure participant knowledge and self-efficacy along with a process for measuring referrals to local screening and treatment programs. Dr. Dawn Silvera-Ndure project is been accessed and utilized globally at the *Walden Dissertations and Doctoral Studies Collection* at *ScholarWorks*@waldenu.edu

Professional Affiliation

1) Dawn is a member of the American Association of Nurse Practitioner. She also earned a Family Nurse Practitioner certification from the American Nurses Credentialing Center (ANCC).

2) Dawn is a proud member of the Honor Society of Nursing, Sigma Theta Tau International (STTI). In July 2019, she was fortunate to be attend and be a presenter at their 30th annual Nursing Research Conference in Calgary, Canada.

3) Dawn is a member of the Caribbean American Nurses Association (CANA) Bronx and Westchester Chapter

Community Service

1) *Friends of Port Maria, NY Chapter, Inc. (FOPM)*

Dawn became a member of the volunteer Organization-Friends of Port Maria, NY Chapter, Inc. (FOPM) in 2016. This organization was founded in 1996. FOPM is a member of the Union of Jamaican Alumni Association (UJAA). The Friends of Port

Maria, New York Chapter, mission is to assist in the overall development of Port Maria and its surroundings communities, as well as to improve the quality of life of the residents. The organization's goal is to create an environment where a satisfactory level of educational, economical, and health care opportunities are available to residents in these communities. FOPM fund raising activities includes its annual dinner dance (May) and annual UJAA Mega raffle (March). Over the years, FOPM had donated hundreds of dollars to schools, daycare, high school students and community events. Dawn was asked to coordinate the organization's very first community health fair. This was achieved with the combined effort of members, friends, family and churches in the community of St. Mary.

To date Dr. Dawn coordinated three annual health fairs in different churches in St. Mary, Jamaica. These churches are: The Emmanuel Baptist Church in Port Maria, the Galina Church of Christ, The Mason Hall Anglican church, and the Preston Hill Roman Catholic Church. Activities performed at the health fair included: Blood pressure screening; Routine Eye testing; Weight checks and BMI calculation; Prostate cancer screening educational information; Health information teaching with information flyers on topics such as: high blood pressure, cholesterol, diabetes, and hypertension. Hundreds of participants attend each year. The participants received bags with useful give away items. Multiple reading glass were given out to each participants, as well as multiple school bags, and books were handed out to the children who attended the health fairs. During the health fair visit, the group also visited the Port Maria hospital and the Infirmary and donated personal items, blood pressure machines, blood sugar monitors, nebulizer machines and other valuable health care products. The 4th annual health Fair is scheduled for August 3rd and 4th 2020 at the Port Maria Primary School

2) *Zoe Ministries Church of New York*

Dawn is a member of Zoe Ministries for over 20 years. Zoe Ministries is headed by Archbishop Bernard Jordan and his wife Pastor Debra Jordan. Dawn was appointed to be a Deacon in 2018. She is an active member of the Zoe Ministries choir, teaches in the children's church on a designated Sunday, serves in the women's ministry by participating in cooking for the food court on Sundays. In addition, Dawn actively participates in the Zoe Ministries annual women conference coordinated by her Pastor Debra Jordan every October (Breast cancer awareness and prevention month). During the conference, Dawn does breast screening prevention education, breast examination, blood pressure screening and blood sugar screening at the conference.

3) *Public Education*

Dawn was guest on **Sweet Riddim.com Radio with Bethynia Palmer**. She spoke on breast cancer prevention screening, Prostate cancer prevention screening and on annual health screening and examination guidelines. Dawn was also a guest on **WOKB Radio Station with Minister Stan Scott**. She spoke on breast cancer prevention screening, Prostate cancer prevention screening and on Annual health screening and examination guidelines.

Education/Affiliation

Doctor of Nursing Practice (DNP): Walden University (November 2016)

FNP Certification: American Nurses Credentialing Center (September 2011)

Member: Sigma Theta Tau International Honor Society of Nursing (May 2010)

Member, American Association of Nurse Practitioners (October 2010)

Family Nurse Practitioner (FNP): Pace University, New York (April 2010)

Master of Science in Nursing (MSN): Lehman College, Bronx New York (May 2002)

Bachelor of Science in Nursing: College of New Rochelle, New York (May

Diploma: Registered General Nurse: University of the West Indies, JWI (June 1983)

With God, I Did It a Memoir by Dr. Dawn Silvera-Ndure, takes readers on a journey through her family history as she shares highlights from her youth while growing up in Jamaica. Dr. Dawn outlines her path as she gives details about her life, legacy, and instinctive desire to push through, even when the odds were against her. Dr. Dawn inspires many while witnessing spiritual growth and transformation in her life and in the lives of those around her.

Author Reviews

"This book is for anyone who needs to know that God still answers prayer. Dawn's life demonstrates what happens when we persevere. By not giving up when the odds were stacked against her, Dr. Dawn Silvera-Ndure comes out victorious with the help of God." Novella Coleman, Author, Poet, Motivational Speaker

With God, I Did It a Memoir by Dr. Dawn Silvera-Ndure inspires many to never stop dreaming. Dr. Dawn's story of pursuing your dreams when there seems to be no hope instills willpower, healing, and wit. Dawn is proof that the legend and legacy of her family will live forever." Valerie Adams, Creative Development Strategist

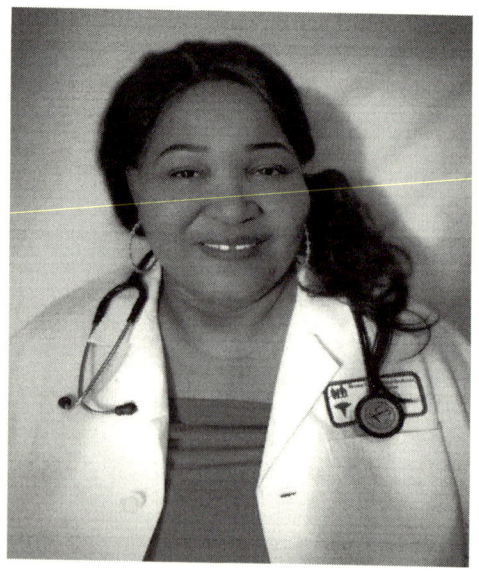